change
your life!
a little book
of big ideas

change
your life!
a little book
of big ideas

COMPILED BY
ALLEN KLEIN

FOREWORD BY
JACK CANFIELD

V!Va
EDITIONS

Published in the United States by Viva Editions, an imprint of Cleis Press Inc., 2246 Sixth Street, Berkeley CA 94710.

Printed in the United States.
Cover design: Scott Idleman
Cover photograph: Teruyuki Yoshimura/Getty Images
Text design: Frank Wiedemann
Cleis logo art: Juana Alicia
First Edition.
10 9 8 7 6 5 4 3 2 1

Library of Congress Cataloging-in-Publication Data

Change your life : a little book of big ideas / compiled by Allen Klein ; foreword by Jack Canfield. -- 1st ed.
     p. cm.
 Includes index.
 ISBN 978-1-57344-407-1 (trade paper : alk. paper)
1. Success--Quotations, maxims, etc. I. Klein, Allen.
BJ1611.2.C485 2010
158--dc22
                                        2010017524

For Dave,
who changed my life
with his deeds—and his words.

CONTENTS

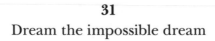

79
Have hope
Help others

93
Keep it light
Know thyself

109
Learn to forgive
Let 'er rip
Life's journey

127
Never give up

FOREWORD

For more than forty-years, I have been helping people manifest their dreams and achieve their maximum potential. As an inspirational speaker and best-selling author, I have provided my audiences and readers with powerful words and thoughts to help them transform their lives. I have come to know that sometimes the simplest words can make a major difference in how people perceive and interact with their world.

This book can make that same difference to you. With a collection of simple yet profound ideas, this little volume of BIG ideas can change your life. Allen Klein, who is also a motivational speaker and best-selling author, has artfully collected words of wisdom from sages throughout the ages—quotations that will make your heart sing, and thoughts that will bring focus, perspective and empowerment to your life.

One of the fun things you can do with this wonderful book is to simply open it to any page and read one of the quotations. Those words just might be the exact words you need to hear that day.

Or you can share this book with someone else—a someone who is celebrating a special occasion such as a graduation, birthday, or anniversary. Or, better yet, give them this book for no reason at all. Your random act of kindness will enrich their life and deepen yours through the simple act of giving.

You can also search the table of contents to find encouraging thoughts on a particular subject you might be struggling with, such as taking the first step, overcoming obstacles, or gathering your courage.

How you make use of this book really doesn't matter. What does matter is *that* you use it. I know it will enrich your life and provide you with big ideas that can make a big difference in your life.

Jack Canfield
Co-author of the *Chicken Soup for the Soul*® series
Santa Barbara, California

INTRODUCTION

It has always amazed me how one simple quotation can change someone's life. I probably shouldn't be surprised because, throughout my life, I have used such things as quotations and affirmations to help me through trying times.

Still, I have received a number of letters from readers who found the perfect quotation in one of my books. It spoke directly to them and altered their life in a very dramatic and profound way.

One young teenager, for example, wrote to tell me that her Dad had given her the quotation book as a gift. She never opened it. Then a couple of months later, her father died. She picked up the book and found a quotation that reminded her of him. She put his picture in the book to mark that page and reads those words of wisdom everyday.

Another woman wrote me that for fifty-five years she had never told anyone about being raped when she was twelve years old. She carried that anger and rage around all those years until she found a quotation about taking back one's power. It has given her strength, hope, and courage. She said, "It has changed my life."

Like the above examples, somewhere in this book there are probably some wise words that call out to you. There is a reason they do. They are your guiding light. They can help you through your trying times, too. And who knows, perhaps even change your life.

Allen Klein
San Francisco

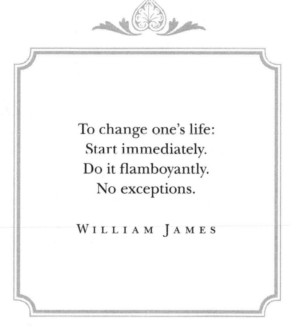

To change one's life:
Start immediately.
Do it flamboyantly.
No exceptions.

WILLIAM JAMES

ACTIONS SPEAK LOUDER THAN WORDS
ALTER YOUR ATTITUDE

Saying is one thing and doing is another.
MONTAIGNE

What you do speaks so loudly that
I cannot hear what you say.
RALPH WALDO EMERSON

Speak little, do much.
BENJAMIN FRANKLIN

We know what a person thinks not when he
tells us what he thinks, but by his actions.
ISAAC BASHEVIS SINGER

Things won are done, joy's soul lies in the doing.
WILLIAM SHAKESPEARE

Get all the education you can, but then, by God, do
something. Don't just stand there; make it happen.
LEE IAOCOCCA

Perhaps the most valuable result of all education is the
ability to make yourself do the thing you have to do,
when it ought to be done, whether you like it or not.
WALTER BAGEHOT

The truth of the matter is that you always know
the right thing to do. The hard part is doing it.
H . NORMAN SCHWARZKOPF

They talk most who have the least to say.
MATTHEW PRIOR

There are very few people who don't become
more interesting when they stop talking.
MARY LOWRY

Noise proves nothing—often a hen who has merely
laid an egg, cackles as if she had laid an asteroid.
MARK TWAIN

The superior man is modest in his speech,
but exceeds in his actions
CONFUCIUS

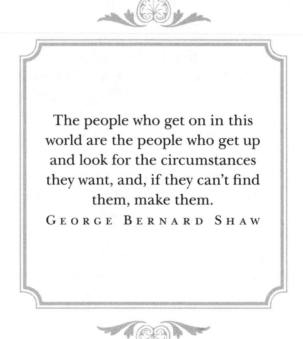

The people who get on in this
world are the people who get up
and look for the circumstances
they want, and, if they can't find
them, make them.

GEORGE BERNARD SHAW

There are two kinds of people: those who don't do what
they want to do, so they write down in a diary about what
they haven't done, and those who haven't time to write
about it because they're out doing it.

RICHARD FLOURNOY
AND LEWIS R. FOSTER

If you have something to do that is worthwhile
doing, don't talk about it...do it.

GEORGE W. BIOUNT

The biggest sin is sitting on your ass.

FLORYNCE R. KENNEDY

Action is the antidote to despair.

JOAN BAEZ

Activity and sadness are incompatible.

CHRISTIAN BOVEE

Action may not always bring happiness;
but there is no happiness without action.

BENJAMIN DISRAELI

All the beautiful sentiments in the world
weigh less than a single lovely action.
J AMES   R USSELL   L OWELL

Words are mere bubbles of water,
but deeds are drops of gold.
C HINESE   PROVERB

Let every action aim solely at the common good.
M ARCUS   A URELIUS

That the moment one definitely commits
oneself, then providence moves too.
G OETHE

It is better to light one candle than to curse the darkness.
C HRISTOPHER   S OCIETY ,   MOTTO

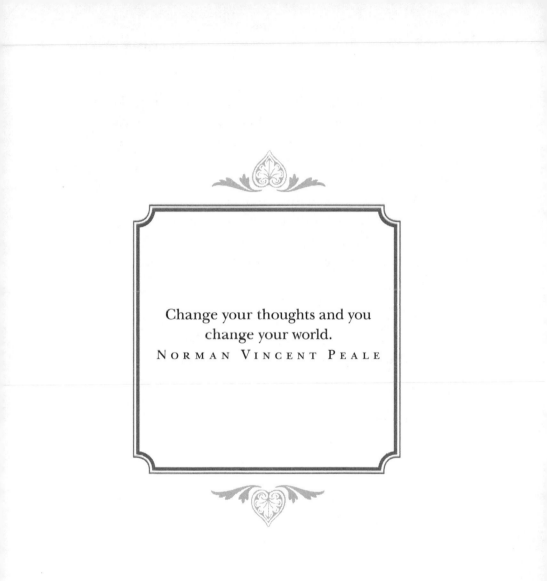

Change your thoughts and you
change your world.
NORMAN VINCENT PEALE

The most powerful thing you can do to change the
world, is to change your own beliefs about the nature
of life, people, reality, to something more positive.

SHAKTI GAWAIN

Watch your thoughts; they become words.
Watch your words; they become actions.
Watch your actions; they become habits.
Watch your habits; they become character.
Watch your character; it becomes your destiny.

FRANK OUTLAW

If you think you can do a thing or
think you can't do a thing, you're right.

HENRY FORD

In the province of the mind, what one believes
to be true either is true or becomes true.

JOHN LILLY

If you want to reach a goal, you must "see the reaching"
in your own mind before you actually arrive at your goal.

ZIG ZIGLAR

The mind is its own place, and in itself, can
make heaven of Hell, and a hell of Heaven.
JOHN MILTON

The last of the human freedoms—to choose one's
attitude in any given set of circumstances,
to choose one's own way.
VIKTOR FRANKL

We cannot choose the things that will happen to us,
but we can choose the attitude we will take toward
anything that happens. Success or failure
depends on your attitude.
ALFRED A. MONTAPERT

Seek out that particular mental attribute which makes
you feel most deeply and vitally alive, along with which
comes the inner voice which says, "This is the real me,"
and when you have found that attitude, follow it.
WILLIAM JAMES

The greatest revolution of our generation is the discovery
that human beings, by changing the inner attitudes of
their minds, can change the outer aspects of their lives.

WILLIAM JAMES

Even a thought, even a possibility
can shatter us and transform us.

FRIEDRICH NIETZSCHE

Two men look out through the same bars;
one sees the mud and one the stars.

FREDERICK LANGBRIDGE

The greatest part of our happiness or misery depends
on our dispositions and not on our circumstances.

MARTHA WASHINGTON

The meaning of things lies not in the things
themselves but in our attitude towards them.

ANTOINE DE SAINT-EXUPÉRY

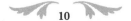

Most people are searching for happiness. They're looking for it. They're trying to find it in someone or something outside of themselves. That's a fundamental mistake. Happiness is something that you are, and it comes from the way you think.

WAYNE DYER

A happy person is not a person in a certain set of circumstances, but rather a person with a certain set of attitudes.

HUGH DOWNS

Remember happiness doesn't depend upon who you are or what you have; it depends solely upon what you think.

DALE CARNEGIE

Ultimately…it's not the stories that determine our choices, but the stories that we continue to choose.

SYLVIA BOORSTEIN

I keep the telephone of my mind open to peace,
harmony, health, love and abundance. Then, whenever
doubts, anxiety, or fear try to call me, they keep getting a
busy signal—and soon they'll forget my number.

E D I T H   A R M S T R O N G

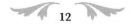

BE GRATEFUL
BELIEVE IN MIRACLES

God gave you a gift of 86,400
seconds today.
Have you used one to say
"thank you"?

W ILLIAM A RTHUR W ARD

Take one thing with another and the world is a pretty
good sort of a world, and it is our duty to make the best
of it and be thankful.
BENJAMIN FRANKLIN

Feeling gratitude and not expressing it
is like wrapping a present and not giving it.
WILLIAM ARTHUR WARD

Gratitude is not only the greatest of virtues,
but the parent of all the others.
CICERO

If the only prayer you say in your whole
life is "thank you," that would suffice.
MEISTER ECKHART

He who receives a benefit with gratitude
repays the first installment on his debt.
SENECA

Appreciation is like an insurance policy.
It has to be renewed every now and then.
DAVE MCINTYRE

Birds sing after a storm; why shouldn't people feel
as free to delight in whatever remains to them?
R O S E   F I T Z G E R A L D   K E N N E D Y

Sunshine is delicious, rain is refreshing,
wind braces us up, snow is exhilarating;
there is really no such thing as bad weather,
only different kinds of good weather.
J O H N   R U S K I N

Not being beautiful was the true blessing....
Not being beautiful forced me to develop my inner
resources. The pretty girl has a handicap to overcome.
G O L D A   M E I R

'Tis better to have loved and lost
than never to have loved at all.
A L F R E D ,   L O R D   T E N N Y S O N

To be upset over what you don't have
is to waste what you do have.
K E N   K E Y E S ,   J R .

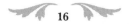

Health is...a blessing that money cannot buy.
IZAAK WALTON

Think of the ills from which you are exempt.
JOSEPH JOUBERT

Count your blessings, not your crosses,
Count your gains, not your losses.
Count your joys instead of your woes,
Count your friends instead of your foes.
Count your health, not your wealth.
OLD PROVERB

He who limps still walks.
STANISLAW LEC

Too many people miss the silver lining
because they're expecting gold.
MAURICE SETTER

If you count all your assets,
you always show a profit.
ROBERT QUILLEN

A piece of the miracle process
has been reserved for each of us.
JIM ROHN

Where there is great love there are miracles.
WILLA CATHER

The world is full of wonders and miracles
but man takes his little hand and covers
his eyes and sees nothing.
ISRAEL BAAL SHEM TOV

Miracles happen to those who believe in them.
BERNARD BERENSON

In any project the important factor is your belief.
Without belief there can be no successful outcome.
WILLIAM JAMES

The thing always happens that you really believe
in; and the belief in a thing makes it happen.

FRANK LLOYD WRIGHT

The only way to live is to accept each minute as an
unrepeatable miracle, which is exactly what it is:
a miracle and unrepeatable.

STORM JAMESON

There are only two ways to live your life.
One is as though nothing is a miracle. The
other is as though everything is a miracle.

ALBERT EINSTEIN

Everything is miraculous. It is miraculous
that one does not melt in one's bath.

PABLO PICASSO

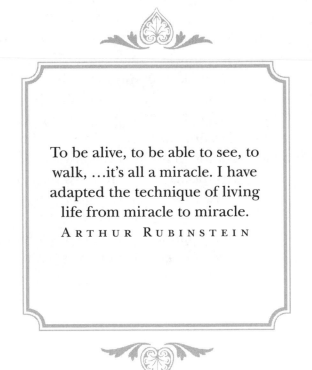

To be alive, to be able to see, to walk, …it's all a miracle. I have adapted the technique of living life from miracle to miracle.

ARTHUR RUBINSTEIN

All the things of the universe are perfect
miracles, each as profound as any.

WALT WHITMAN

That greatest miracle of all, the human being.

MARYA MANNES

There is a giant asleep within every man.
When that giant awakes, miracles happen.

FREDERICK FAUST

Miracles, in the sense of phenomena
we cannot explain, surround us on every hand:
life itself is the miracle of miracles.

GEORGE BERNARD SHAW

We couldn't conceive of a miracle
if none had ever happened.

LIBBIE FUDIM

Expect a miracle!

ORAL ROBERTS

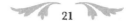

CULTIVATE KINDNESS & COMPASSION

No one cares how much you
know, until they know how
much you care.

DON SWARTZ

Kindness is the language which the deaf can hear and the blind can see.

MARK TWAIN

One kind word can warm three winter months.

JAPANESE PROVERB

Kind words can be short and easy to speak, but their echoes are truly endless.

MOTHER TERESA

Kindness is a hard thing to give away; it keeps coming back to the giver.

RALPH SCOTT

Kindness is never wasted. If it has no effect on the recipient, at least it benefits the bestower.

S. H. SIMMONS

You have it easily in your power to increase the sum total of this world's happiness now. How? By giving a few words of sincere appreciation to someone who is lonely or discouraged. Perhaps you will forget tomorrow the kind words you say today, but the recipient may cherish them over a lifetime.

D A L E   C A R N E G I E

I expect to pass through life but once. If therefore, there be any kindness I can show, or any good thing I can do to any fellow being, let me do it now, and not defer or neglect it, as I shall not pass this way again.

W I L L I A M   P E N N

Life is not so short but that there is always time enough for courtesy.

R A L P H   W A L D O   E M E R S O N

A pat on the back, though only a few vertebrae removed from a kick in the pants, is miles ahead in results.

B E N N E T T   C E R F

If you step on people in this life, you're going to come
back as a cockroach.

WILLIE DAVIS

Until you have learned to be tolerant with those who do
not always agree with you; until you have cultivated the
habit of saying some kind word of those whom you do not
admire; until you have formed the habit of looking for
the good instead of the bad there is in others, you will be
neither successful nor happy.

NAPOLEAN HILL

Keep in mind that the true meaning
of an individual is how he treats a person
who can do him absolutely no good.

ANN LANDERS

Be nice to people on your way up because
you'll meet them on your way down.

WILSON MIZNER

Never look down on anybody
unless you're helping them up.

JESSE JACKSON

The individual is capable of both great compassion and
great indifference. He has it within his means to nourish
the former and outgrow the latter.

NORMAN COUSINS

When a man has compassion for others,
God has compassion for him.

TALMUD

Compassion for yourself
translates into compassion for others.

SUKI JAY MUNSELL

It's only in our minds that we are separate
from the rest of the world.

GAY LUCE

Until he extends the circle of his compassion to all
living things, man will not himself find peace.

ALBERT SCHWEITZER

I think the purpose of life is to be useful, to be responsible, to be honorable, to be compassionate. It is, after all, to matter: to count, to stand for something, to have made some difference that you lived at all.

LEO ROSTEN

Often the most loving thing we can do when a friend is in pain is to share the pain—to be there even when we have nothing to offer except our presence and even when being there is painful to ourselves.

M. SCOTT PECK

Shall we make a new rule of life from tonight: always to try to be a little kinder than is necessary?

J. M. BARRIE

That old law about "an eye for and eye" leaves everybody blind.

MARTIN LUTHER KING, JR.

DREAM THE IMPOSSIBLE DREAM

"One can't believe impossible things." "I daresay you
haven't had much practice," said the Queen.
"When I was your age, I always did it for half-an-hour a
day. Why, sometimes I've believed as many as
six impossible things before breakfast."

LEWIS CARROLL

It is difficult to say what is impossible,
for the dream of yesterday is the hope of today and the
reality of tomorrow.

ROBERT H. GODDARD

All big things in this world are done by people who are
naive and have an idea that is obviously impossible.

FRANK RICHARDS

Man is so made that whenever anything fires his soul,
impossibilities vanish.

LA FONTAINE

A dream is in the mind of the believer and in
the hands of the doer. You are not given a dream
without being given the power to make it come true.

ANONYMOUS

Don't be afraid of the space between your dreams
and reality. If you can dream it, you can make it so.
BELVA DAVIS

If one advances confidently in the direction of his
dreams and endeavors to live the life
which he has imagined, he will meet with
a success unexpected in common hours.
HENRY DAVID THOREAU

If you have enough fantasies, you're ready,
in the event that something happens.
SHEILA BALLANTYNE

Hitch your wagon to a star.
RALPH WALDO EMERSON

Reach high, for stars lie hidden in your soul.
Dream deep, for every dream precedes the goal.
PAMELA VAULL STARR

Follow your bliss.
JOSEPH CAMPBELL

My parents taught me that I could do anything I wanted
and I have always believed it to be true. Add a clear idea
of what inspires you, dedicate your energies to its pursuit,
and there is no knowing what you can achieve,
particularly if others are inspired by your dream
and offer their help.

PETE GOSS

To live on purpose, follow your heart
and live your dreams.

MARCIA WIEDER

Within your heart, keep one still,
secret spot where dreams may go.

LOUISE DRISCOLL

The future belongs to those who believe
in the beauty of their dreams.

ELEANOR ROOSEVELT

All our dreams can come true—
if you have the courage to pursue them.

WALT DISNEY

Far away there in the sunshine are my highest
aspirations. I may not reach them, but I can look up and
see their beauty, believe in them, and try to follow them.

LOUISA MAY ALCOTT

Everything starts as somebody's daydream.

LARRY NIVEN

Dreams are extremely important.
You can't do it unless you imagine it.

GEORGE LUCAS

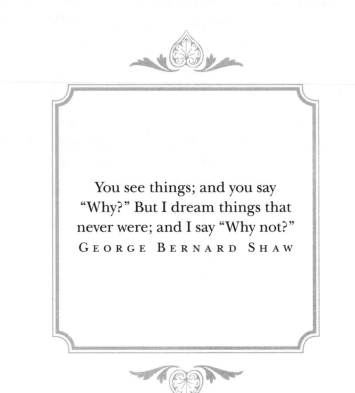

You see things; and you say
"Why?" But I dream things that
never were; and I say "Why not?"

GEORGE BERNARD SHAW

The Wright brothers flew right through
the smoke screen of impossibility.
CHARLES F. KETTERING

There comes a time in a man's life when to get where he
has to go—if there are no doors or windows—he walks
through a wall.
BERNARD MALAMUD

Believe in something larger than yourself.
BARBARA BUSH

As long as you're going to think anyway, think big.
DONALD TRUMP

Doctors and scientists said that breaking the four-minute
mile was impossible, that one would die in the attempt.
Thus, when I got up from the track after collapsing at the
finish line, I figured I was dead.
ROGER BANNISTER

Always listen to experts. They'll tell you
what can't be done and why. Then do it.
ROBERT HEINLEIN

The ark was built by amateurs and the
Titanic by experts. Don't wait for experts.

MURRAY COHEN

I owe my success to having listened respectfully
to the very best advice, and then going away
and doing the exact opposite.

G. K. CHESTERTON

Most people never run far enough on their first wind
to find out if they've got a second. Give your dreams all
you've got, and you'll be amazed at the energy
that comes out of you.

WILLIAM JAMES

Why not go out on a limb? Isn't that where the fruit is?

FRANK SCULLY

Whatever you can do, or dream you can—begin
it. Boldness has genius, power, and magic in it.

GOETHE

There are no rules of architecture
for a castle in the clouds.
G . K . CHESTERTON

If you have built castles in the air, your work need not be
lost; that is where they should be. Now put the founda-
tions under them.
HENRY DAVID THOREAU

EMBRACE CHANGE
ENJOY TODAY

To exist is to change, to change is to mature,
to mature is to go on creating oneself endlessly.
HENRI BERGSON

Even if you're on the right track,
you'll get run over if you just sit there.
WILL ROGERS

One must never lose time in vainly regretting the past
or in complaining against the changes which cause us
discomfort, for change is the essence of life.
ANATOLE FRANCE

We must change in order to survive.
PEARL BAILEY

When you're through changing, you're through.
BRUCE BARTON

Since we live in a changing universe, why do men oppose change? ...If a rock is in the way, the root of a tree will change its direction. The dumbest animals try to adapt themselves to changed conditions. Even a rat will change its tactics to get a piece of cheese.

MELVIN B. TOLSON

Change is a challenge and an opportunity, not a threat

PRINCE PHILLIP OF ENGLAND

Change is often rejuvenating, invigorating, fun...and necessary.

LYNN POVICH

The first step toward change is acceptance.... Change is not something you do, it's something you allow.

WILL GARCIA

All changes, even the most longed for, have their melancholy, for what we leave behind us is a part of ourselves; we must die to one life before we can enter into another.

ANATOLE FRANCE

Each new season grows from the leftovers
from the past. That is the essence of change,
and change is the basic law.

H A L   B O R L A N D

Everything is connected...
no one thing can change by itself.

P A U L   H A W K E N

Be the change that you want
to see in the world.

MAHATMA GANDHI

If you don't like the way the world is, you
change it. You have an obligation to change it.
MARIAN WRIGHT EDELMAN

Will you be the rock
that redirects the course of the river?
CLAIRE NUER

The world will not change until we do.
JIM WALLIS

When we are no longer able to change a
situation…we are challenged to change ourselves.
VIKTOR FRANKL

Never underestimate your power to change yourself:
never overestimate your power to change others.
H. JACKSON BROWN, JR.

Things don't change. You change your way of looking,
that's all.
CARLOS CASTANEDA

46

Everything flows, nothing stays still.
HERACLITUS

Be Here Now
RAM DASS

And if not now, when?
TALMUD

Life is a great and wondrous mystery,
and the only thing we know that we have for sure
is what is right here right now. Don't miss it.
LEO BUSCAGLIA

Yesterday is a canceled check; tomorrow is a promissory
note; today is the only cash you have—so spend it wisely.
KAY LYONS

How we spend our days is, of course,
how we spend our lives.

ANNIE DILLARD

The only history that is worth a tinker's
damn is the history we make today.

HENRY FORD

I have everything I need to enjoy my here and now—
unless I am letting my consciousness be
dominated by demands and expectations
based on the dead past or the imagined future.

KEN KEYES, JR.

You can clutch the past so tightly to your chest that
it leaves your arms too full to embrace the present.

JAN GLIDEWELL

He who lives in the present lives in eternity.

LUDWIG WITTGENSTEIN

Tomorrow's life is too late. Live today.

MARCUS VALERIUS MARTIAL

Today is the first day of the rest of your life.
CHARLES DEDERICH

It's not that "today is the first day of the rest of
my life," but that now is all there is of my life.
HUGH PRATHER

Yesterday is ashes; tomorrow wood.
Only today does the fire burn brightly.
ESKIMO SAYING

The past is a bucket of ashes, so live not in your
yesterdays, nor just for tomorrow,
but in the here and now.
CARL SANDBURG

The past cannot be regained, although we can learn
from it; the future is not yet ours even though we
must plan for it.... Time is now. We have only today.
CHARLES HUMMELL

This is the day which the Lord has made. Let us rejoice
and be glad in it.
PSALMS 118:24

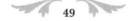

This day is all that is good and fair. It is too dear, with its
hopes and invitations, to waste a moment
on the yesterdays.

R A L P H W A L D O E M E R S O N

There are two days in the week about which and upon
which I never worry.... One of these days is Yesterday....
And the other day I do not worry about is Tomorrow.

R O B E R T J O N E S B U R D E T T E

I live now and only now, and I will do what
I want to do this moment and not what
I decided was best for me yesterday.

H U G H P R A T H E R

I have learned to live each day as it comes and not to
borrow trouble by dreading tomorrow. It is the
dark menace of the future that makes cowards of us.

D O R O T H Y D I X

We know nothing of tomorrow; our
business is to be good and happy today.

S Y D N E Y S M I T H

You don't save a pitcher for tomorrow.
Tomorrow it may rain.
LEO DUROCHER

Don't put off for tomorrow what you can do today,
because if you enjoy it today you can do it again
tomorrow.
JAMES A. MICHENER

Some people are making such thorough preparation for
rainy days that they aren't enjoying today's sunshine.
WILLIAM FEATHER

So never let a cloudy day ruin your sunshine, for
even if you can't see it, the sunshine is still there,
inside of you ready to shine when you will let it.
AMY PITZELE

If you let yourself be absorbed completely, if you
surrender completely to the moments as they pass,
you live more richly those moments.
ANNE MORROW LINDBERGH

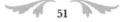

I can feel guilty about the past, apprehensive about
the future, but only in the present can I act.
The ability to be in the present moment is a major
component of mental wellness.

ABRAHAM MASLOW

We have only this moment, sparkling like a star
in our hand...and melting like a snowflake.
Let us use it before it is too late.

MARIE BEYNON RAY

Love the moment, and the energy of that moment
will spread beyond all boundaries.

CORITA KENT

Each day comes bearing its own
gifts. Untie the ribbons.

RUTH ANN SCHABACKER

Normal day, let me be aware of the treasure you are.

MARY JEAN IRION

There is no such thing in anyone's life
as an unimportant day.

ALEXANDER WOOLLCOTT

I thank you God for this most amazing day; for the
leaping greenly spirits of trees and a blue true dream
of sky; and for everything which is natural
which is infinite which is yes.

E. E. CUMMINGS

Write in your heart that every day is
the best day of the year.

RALPH WALDO EMERSON

If we are ever to enjoy life, now is the time,
not tomorrow or next year....
Today should always be our most wonderful day.

THOMAS DREIER

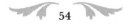

Surpassingly lively, precious days.
What is there to say except: here they are.
Sifting through my fingers like sand.
JOYCE CAROL OATES

Life is all memory except for the one present moment
that goes by so quick you can hardly catch it going.
TENNESSEE WILLIAMS

Light tomorrow with today.
ELIZABETH BARRETT BROWNING

Whether it's the best of times or the worst
of times, it's the only time we've got.
ART BUCHWALD

FORGET FAILURE

Forget past mistakes. Forget failures. Forget everything
except what you're going to do now and do it.
WILLIAM DURANT

People who soar are those who refuse to sit back, sigh
and wish things would change. They neither complain of
their lot nor passively dream of some distant ship coming
in. Rather, they visualize in their minds that they are not
quitters; they will not allow life's circumstances to push
them down and hold them under.
CHARLES R. SWINDOLL

Don't wait for extraordinary opportunities.
Seize common occasions and make them great.
ORISON S. MARDEN

Far better it is to dare mighty things, to win glorious
triumphs, even though checkered by failure, than to take
rank with those poor spirits who neither enjoy much nor
suffer much, because they live in the gray twilight that
knows not victory or defeat.
THEODORE ROOSEVELT

What is defeat? Nothing but education, nothing
but the first step toward something better.
W E N D E L L   P H I L L I P S

Mistakes are portals of discovery.
J A M E S   J O Y C E

There is nothing final about a mistake,
except its being taken as final.
P H Y L L I S   B O T T O M E

To lose is to learn.
A N O N Y M O U S

Disappointment to a noble soul is what cold water means
to burning metal; it strengthens, tempers, intensifies,
but never destroys it.
E L I Z A   T A B O R

I have missed more than 9000 shots in my career. I have lost almost 300 games. On 26 occasions I have been entrusted to take the game's winning shot…and missed. And I have failed over and over and over again in my life. And that is why…I succeed.

MICHAEL JORDAN

You miss 100% of the shots you don't take.

WAYNE GRETZKY

Ninety-nine percent of the failures come from people who have the habit of making excuses.

GEORGE WASHINGTON CARVER

If you're gonna be a failure,
at least be one at something you enjoy.

SYLVESTER STALLONE

Failure is delay, but not defeat. It is a temporary detour, not a dead-end street.

WILLIAM ARTHUR WARD

Being defeated is often a temporary condition.
Giving up is what makes it permanent.
MARILYN VOS SAVANT

Failure is impossible.
SUSAN B. ANTHONY

Failure is the condiment that gives success its flavor.
TRUMAN CAPOTE

Failure…is, in a sense, the highway to success, inas-
much as every discovery of what is false leads us to seek
earnestly after what is true, and every fresh experience
points out some form of error which we shall afterward
carefully avoid.
JOHN KEATS

Good people are good because they've come to wisdom
through failure. We get very little wisdom from success,
you know.
WILLIAM SAROYAN

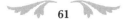

No experiment is ever a complete failure.
It can always be used as a bad example.
PAUL DICKSON

I wasn't afraid to fail.
Something good always comes out of failure.
ANNE BAXTER

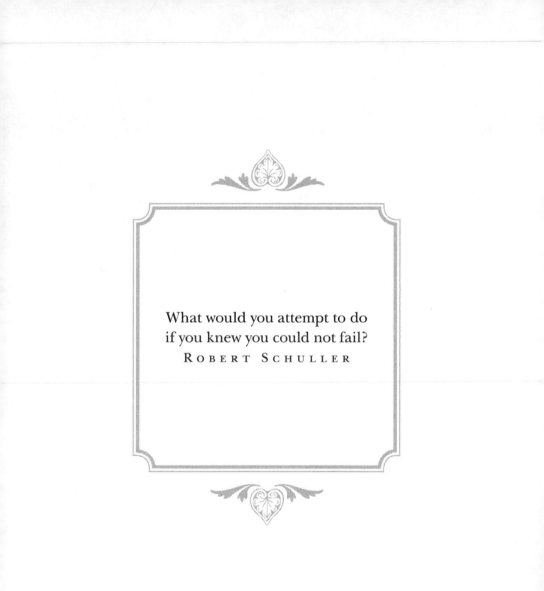

What would you attempt to do
if you knew you could not fail?

ROBERT SCHULLER

GATHER YOUR COURAGE
GROW OLD GRACEFULLY

Courage is grace under pressure.
ERNEST HEMINGWAY

Courage is fear that has said its prayers.
RUTH FISHEL

Courage is not the towering oak that sees storms come
and go; it is the fragile blossom that opens in the snow.
ALICE M. SWAIM

Courage takes many forms. There is physical courage,
there is moral courage. Then there is a still higher type
of courage—the courage to brave pain, to live with it,
to never let others know of it and to still
find joy in life; to wake up in the morning
with an enthusiasm for the day ahead.
HOWARD COSELL

You gain strength, courage, and confidence by
every experience in which you really stop to
look fear in the face. You are able to say to yourself,
"I lived through this horror.
I can take the next thing that comes along."
ELEANOR ROOSEVELT

What is more mortifying than to feel that you have
missed the plum for want of courage to shake the tree?
LOGAN PEARSALL SMITH

You can't be brave if you've only had
wonderful things happen to you.
MARY TYLER MOORE

Oh God, give us serenity to accept what cannot be
changed; courage to change what should be changed,
and wisdom to distinguish the one from the other.
REINHOLD NIEBUHR

Grant me the courage not to give up
even though I think it is hopeless.
CHESTER W. NIMITZ

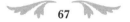

Courage is not the absence of
fear, but the mastery of it.
MARK TWAIN

The only thing we have to fear is fear itself.

FRANKLIN D. ROOSEVELT

Feel the fear, and do it anyway.

SUSAN JEFFERS

Confronting your fears and allowing yourself the right to be human can, paradoxically, make you a far happier and more productive person.

DAVID M. BURNS

Fear is a question. What are you afraid of and why?
Our fears are a treasure house of self knowledge
if we explore them.

MARILYN FERGUSON

Whatever you do, you need courage. Whatever course you decide upon, there is always someone to tell you you are wrong. There are always difficulties arising which tempt you to believe that your critics are right. To map out a course of action and follow it to the end requires some of the same courage which a soldier needs.

RALPH WALDO EMERSON

To face despair and not give in to it, that's courage.
TED KOPPEL

The greatest test of courage is to bear defeat
without losing heart.
ROBERT G. INGERSOLL

There are days when you don't have a
song in your heart. Sing anyway.
EMORY AUSTIN

The only courage that matters is the kind
that gets you from one moment to the next.
MIGNON MCLAUGHLIN

To be courageous means to be afraid but to go a little
step forward anyway.
BEVERLY SMITH

The bravest thing you can do when you are not
brave is to profess courage and act accordingly.
CORRA MAY WHITE HARRIS

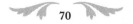

Life shrinks or expands in proportion to one's courage.
ANAÏS NIN

Courage is very important.
Like a muscle, it is strengthened by use.
RUTH GORDON

Courage is contagious. When a brave man takes
a stand, the spines of others are often stiffened.
BILLY GRAHAM

If you carry your childhood with you,
you never become older.
ABRAHAM SUTZKEVER

Growing old is manditory; growing up is optional.
BUMPER STICKER

You're never too old to do goofy stuff.
WARD CLEAVER, "LEAVE IT TO BEAVER"

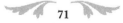

Never think any oldish thoughts.
It's oldish thoughts that make a person old.
JAMES A. FARLEY

Cancer, schmancer—as long as you're healthy.
JEWISH SAYING

As for me, except for an occasional
heart attack, I feel as young as I ever did.
ROBERT BENCHLEY

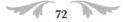

You can't help getting older,
but you don't have to get old.

GEORGE BURNS

You're never too old to become younger.
MAE WEST

I don't know what the big deal is about old age.
Old people who shine from inside
look 10 to 20 years younger.
DOLLY PARTON

Wrinkles should merely indicate
where the smiles have been.
MARK TWAIN

Nothing is more beautiful
than cheerfulness in an old face.
JEAN PAUL FRIEDRICH RICHTER

I never feel age.... If you have creative work,
you don't have age or time.
LOUISE NEVELSON

Nobody grows old by merely living a number of years.
People grow old only by deserting their ideals. Years may
wrinkle the skin, but to give up interest wrinkles the soul.

DOUGLAS MACARTHUR

It is not the years in your life
but the life in your years that counts.

ADLAI STEVENSON

The best part of the art of living
is to know how to grow old gracefully.

ERIC HOFFER

Old age has a great sense of calm and freedom.
When the passions have relaxed their hold, you
have escaped not from one master but from many.

PLATO

The older I get, the greater power I seem to
have to help the world; I am like a snowball—
the further I am rolled, the more I gain.

SUSAN B. ANTHONY

I've always been proud of my age. I think people should
be proud they've been around long enough to have
learned something.

F R A N C E S   M O O R E   L A P P É

A new broom sweeps clean,
but an old one knows the corners.

E N G L I S H   S A Y I N G

In youth we learn, in old age we understand.

M A R I E   V O N   E B N E R - E S C H E N B A C H

One advantage in growing older is that
you can stand for more and fall for less.

M O N T A   C R A N E

Age is opportunity no less
Than youth itself, though in another dress,
And as the evening twilight fades away
The sky is filled with stars, invisible by day.

H E N R Y   W A D S W O R T H   L O N G F E L L O W

Old age has its pleasure, which, though different,
are not less than the pleasures of youth.
W. SOMERSET MAUGHAM

There's many a good tune played on an old fiddle.
SAMUEL BUTLER

Grow along with me!
The best is yet to be,
The last of life, for which the first was made.
ROBERT BROWNING

I have no romantic feelings about age. Either you are
interesting at any age or you are not. There is nothing
particularly interesting about being old—
or being young, for that matter.
KATHARINE HEPBURN

After thirty, a body has a mind of its own.
BETTE MIDLER

Retirement at sixty-five is ridiculous.
When I was sixty-five, I still had pimples.
GEORGE BURNS

I'm saving that rocker for the day
when I feel as old as I really am.
DWIGHT D. EISENHOWER

If you rest, you rust.
HELEN HAYES

As you get older, don't slow down.
Speed up. There's less time left!
MALCOM FORBES

The joy of being older is that in one's life, one can,
towards the end of the run, over-act appallingly.
QUENTIN CRISP

Live your life and forget your age.
FRANK BERING

HAVE HOPE
HELP OTHERS

To travel hopefully is a better thing than to arrive.
ROBERT LOUIS STEVENSON

Hope is the feeling you have
that the feeling you have isn't permanent.
JEAN KERR

Where there's life, there's hope.
TERENCE

If it were not for hopes, the heart would break.
THOMAS FULLER

They say a person needs just three things to be truly
happy in this world. Someone to love, something to do,
and something to hope for.
TOM BODETT

The important thing is not that we can live on hope
alone, but that life is not worth living without it.
HARVEY MILK

Man can live about forty days without food, about three
days without water, about eight minutes without air...but
only for one second without hope.

H A L   L I N D S E Y

Hope, the best comfort of our imperfect condition.

E D W A R D   G I B B O N

Hope, like the gleaming taper's light,
Adorns and cheers our way;
And still, as darker grows the night,
Emits a brighter ray.

O L I V E R   G O L D S M I T H

Hope sees the invisible, feels the intangible,
and achieves the impossible.

A N O N Y M O U S

Hope is a good thing—maybe the best
thing, and no good thing every dies.

S T E P H E N   K I N G

Look not thou down but up!

R O B E R T   B R O W N I N G

The hopeful man sees success where others see failure,
sunshine where others see shadows and storm.
ORISON S. MARDEN

If winter comes, can spring be far behind?
PERCY BYSSHE SHELLEY

Flowers grow out of dark moments.
CORITA KENT

Hope is the thing with feathers that perches in the soul
and sings the tune without words and never stops at all.
EMILY DICKINSON

The gift we can offer others is so simple a thing as hope.
DANIEL BERRIGAN

There are no hopeless situations; there are only
people who have grown hopeless about them.
CLARE BOOTHE LUCE

There is no medicine like hope, no incentive so great,
and no tonic so powerful as expectation
of something tomorrow.
ORISON S. MARDEN

There is one thing which gives radiance to everything.
It is the idea of something around the corner.
G. K. CHESTERTON

After all, tomorrow is another day.
MARGARET MITCHELL

Tomorrow is the most important thing in life. Comes into
us at midnight very clean. It's perfect when it arrives and
it puts itself in our hands. It hopes we've learned something from yesterday.
JOHN WAYNE

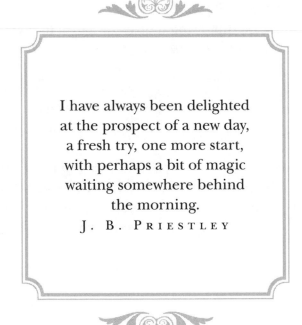

I have always been delighted
at the prospect of a new day,
a fresh try, one more start,
with perhaps a bit of magic
waiting somewhere behind
the morning.

J. B. PRIESTLEY

Just remember—when you think all is lost,
the future remains.
B O B   G O D D A R D

Keep hope alive!
J E S S E   J A C K S O N

We live very close together. So, our prime purpose in this
life is to help others. And if you can't help them, at least
don't hurt them.
D A L A I   L A M A

No one is useless in this world who lightens the burden of
it for anyone else.
C H A R L E S   D I C K E N S

God has given us two hands, one to
receive with and the other to give with.
B I L L Y   G R A H A M

Remember, if you ever need a helping hand, you'll find one at the end of your arm…. As you grow older you will discover that you have two hands. One for helping yourself, the other for helping others.

AUDREY HEPBURN

Giving is the highest expression of power.

VIVIAN GREENE

You have not done enough, you have never done enough, so long as it is still possible that you have something to contribute.

DAG HAMMARSKJÖLD

We ourselves feel that what we are doing is just a drop in the ocean. But the ocean would be less because of that missing drop.

MOTHER TERESA

There is no exercise better for the heart than reaching down and lifting people up.

JOHN ANDREW HOLMES, JR.

When a man is singing and cannot lift his voice, and
another comes and sings with him, another who can lift
his voice, the first will be able to lift his voice, too. That is
the secret of the bond between spirits.

HASIDIC SAYING

Whether or not we realize it, each of us has within
us the ability to set some kind of example for people.
Knowing this would you rather be the one known for
being the one who encouraged others, or the one who
inadvertently discouraged those around you?

JOSH HINDS

A life isn't significant except for its impact on other lives.

JACKIE ROBINSON

Somewhere out there is a unique place
for you to help others—a unique life role
for you to fill that only you can fill.

THOMAS KINKADE

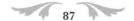

The sole meaning of life is to serve humanity.
LEO TOLSTOY

Long-range studies imply that doing something with
other people, especially something for them, is the
most powerful of all stimuli to longevity and health.
JON POPPY

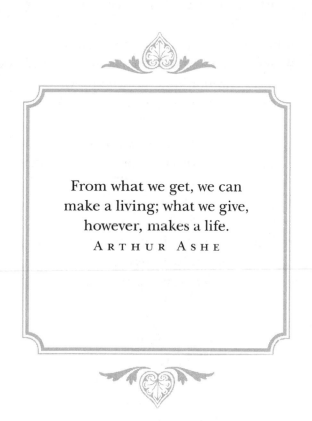

From what we get, we can
make a living; what we give,
however, makes a life.

ARTHUR ASHE

Service is the rent that you pay for room on this earth.
SHIRLEY CHISHOLM

Whoever renders service to many puts himself in line for greatness—great wealth, great return, great satisfaction, great reputation, and great joy.
JIM ROHN

One thing I know: the only ones among you who will be really happy are those who will have sought and found how to serve.
ALBERT SCHWEITZER

There is no happiness in having or in getting, but only in giving.
HENRY DRUMMOND

You give but little when you give of your possessions. It is when you give of yourself that you truly give.
KAHLIL GIBRAN

The miracle is this—the more we share, the more we have.
LEONARD NIMOY

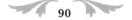

...the ones that give, get back in kind.
PAM DURBAN

In helping others, we shall help ourselves,
for whatever good we give out completes the circle
and comes back to us.
FLORA EDWARDS

The world is good natured to people
who are good natured.
WILLIAM MAKEPEACE THACKERAY

It is one of the most beautiful compensations of this life
that you cannot sincerely try to help another without
helping yourself.
RALPH WALDO EMERSON

By helping yourself, you are helping mankind.
By helping mankind, you are helping yourself.
That's the law of all spiritual progress.
CHRISTOPHER ISHERWOOD

If you always give, you will always have.
CHINESE PROVERB

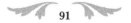

When people are serving, life is no longer meaningless.
JOHN GARDNER

Do things for others and you'll find your
self-consciousness evaporating like morning dew
on a Missouri cornfield in July.
DALE CARNEGIE

Giving opens the way to receiving.
FLORENCE SCOVEL SHINN

To serve is beautiful, but only if it is done
with joy and a whole heart and a free mind.
PEARL S. BUCK

You have not lived a perfect day, even though you have
earned your money, unless you have done something
for someone who will never be able to repay you.
RUTH SMELTZER

Real charity doesn't care if it's tax-deductible or not.
DAN BENNETT

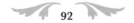

KEEP IT LIGHT
KNOW THYSELF

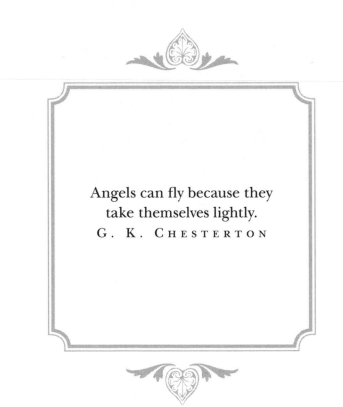

Angels can fly because they
take themselves lightly.

G. K. CHESTERTON

Let your life lightly dance on the edges
of time like dew on the tip of a leaf.
RABINDRANATH TAGORE

The one important thing I've learned over the years
is the difference between taking one's work seriously
and one's self seriously. The first is imperative;
the second is disastrous.
DAME MARGOT FONTEYN

Do not take life too seriously.
You will never get out of it alive.
ELBERT HUBBARD

Sit loosely in the saddle of life.
ROBERT LOUIS STEVENSON

The bird of paradise alights only upon
the hand that does not grasp.
JOHN BERRY

The willow which bends to the tempest, often escapes
better than the oak which resists it; and so in great
calamities, it sometimes happens that light and
frivolous spirits recover their elasticity and presence
of mind sooner than those of a loftier character.

WALTER SCOTT

Let us be of good cheer, remembering that the misfortunes hardest to bear are those which never happen.

JAMES RUSSELL LOWELL

The game is supposed to be fun.
If you have a bad day, don't worry about it.
You can't expect to get a hit every game.

YOGI BERRA

We live in an ironic society where even play is turned into
work. But the highest existence is not work; the highest
level of existence is play.

CONRAD HYERS

Can you imagine experiencing the world as a great
sandbox given for us to play in like we did as children? As
we play, we can also open ourselves to the exploration of
our edges, always creating new adventures of
self-exploration as we let go of old, out-dated
beliefs about ourselves.
JUDITH-ANNETTE MILBURN

Life begins as a quest of the child for the man and
ends as a journey by the man to rediscover the child.
LAURENS VAN DER POST

If my heart can become pure and simple like that
of a child, I think there probably can be
no greater happiness than this.
KITARO NISHIDA

Great is the man who has not lost his childlike heart.
MENCIUS

To bring up a child in the way he should go,
travel that way yourself once in a while.
JOSH BILLINGS

All animals except man know that
the principal business of life is to enjoy it.

SAMUEL BUTLER

Blessed is he who has learned to laugh at himself,
for he shall never cease to be entertained.

JOHN POWELL

You should treat all disasters as if they were trivialities
but never treat a triviality as if it were a disaster.

QUENTIN CRISP

There are some things so serious
you have to laugh at them.

NIELS BOHR

Jokes are better than war. Even the most aggressive
jokes are better than the least aggressive wars. Even
the longest jokes are better than the shortest wars.

GEORGE MIKES

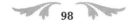

I live by this credo: have a little laugh and look around
you for happiness instead of sadness. Laughter has always
brought me out of unhappy situations. Even in your
darkest moment, you usually can find something to laugh
about if you try hard enough.

RED SKELTON

Happiness is not a state to arrive at,
but a manner of traveling.

MARGARET LEE RUNBECK

To be happy, drop the words "if only" and substitute
instead the words "next time."

SMILEY BLANTON

Man is unhappy because he doesn't know he's happy.
If anyone finds out he'll become happy at once.

FYODOR DOSTOYEVSKY

Make up your mind to be happy.
Learn to find pleasure in simple things.

ROBERT LOUIS STEVENSON

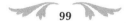

As long as I have food and the remote control, I'm happy.
MARGIE KLEIN
(author's mother)

Sometimes in your life you will go on a journey.
It will be the longest journey you have ever taken.
It is the journey to find yourself.
KATHERINE SHARP

Though we travel the world over to find the
beautiful, we must carry it with us or we find it not.
RALPH WALDO EMERSON

The questions which one asks oneself begin, at last,
to illuminate the world, and become one's key
to the experience of others.
JAMES BALDWIN

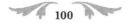

When one is out of touch with oneself,
one cannot touch others.

ANNE MORROW LINDBERGH

There is only one corner of the universe you can be
certain of improving, and that's your own self.

ALDOUS HUXLEY

Nothing can bring you peace but yourself.

RALPH WALDO EMERSON

If a man wants to be of the greatest possible value to his
fellow-creatures, let him begin the long, solitary task of
perfecting himself.

ROBERTSON DAVIES

Every day, in every way, I'm getting better and better.

EMILE COUÉ

Your only obligation in any lifetime
is to be true to yourself.

RICHARD BACH

What you think of yourself is much more
important than what others think of you.

SENECA

No one can make you feel inferior without your consent.

ELEANOR ROOSEVELT

Don't undermine your worth by comparing
yourself with others. It is because we are different
that each of us is special.

BRIAN DYSON

Don't compromise yourself. You are all you've got.

JANIS JOPLIN

We have a mental block inside us that stops
us from earning more than we think we are worth.
If we want to earn more in reality,
we have to upgrade our self-concept.

BRIAN TRACY

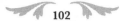

What you discover on your own is always
more exiting than what someone else discovers for you—
it's like the difference between romantic love
and an arranged marriage.
TERENCE RAFFERTY

Know how to live within yourself: there is in your soul a
whole world of mysterious and enchanted thoughts; they
will be drowned by the noise without; daylight will drive
them away; listen to their singing and be silent.
FYODOR TYUTCHEV

All the wonders you seek are within yourself.
SIR THOMAS BROWNE

I celebrate myself, and sing myself.
WALT WHITMAN

Know yourself. Don't accept
your dog's admiration as
conclusive evidence that you
are wonderful.

A N N   L A N D E R S

Your vision will become clear only when you can look
into your own heart. Who looks outside, dreams; who
looks inside, awakes.

CARL JUNG

Until you make peace with who you are,
you'll never be content with what you have.

DORIS MORTMAN

How many cares one loses when one decides
not to be something but to be someone.

COCO CHANEL

The important thing is this: to be able at any moment
to sacrifice what we are for what we could become.

CHARLES DU BOS

We are each gifted in a unique and important way.
It is our privilege and our adventure to discover
our own special light.

MARY DUNBAR

We are the choices we make.

MERYL STREEP

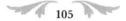

Use what talents you possess; the woods would be very
silent if no birds sang except those that sang best.
HENRY VAN DYKE

Everyone has talent. What is rare is the courage
to follow the talent to the dark place where it leads.
ERICA JONG

Follow your instincts.
That is where true wisdom manifests itself.
OPRAH WINFREY

Self-pity gets you nowhere. One must have the adven-
turous daring to accept oneself as a bundle of possibili-
ties and undertake the most interesting game in the
world—making the most of one's best.
HARRY EMERSON FOSDICK

The ultimate goal should be
doing your best and enjoying it.
PEGGY FLEMING

I've always tried to do my best on the ball field. I can't do any more than that. I always try to give one hundred percent; and if my team loses, I come back and give one hundred percent the next day.

JESSE BARFIELD

Think of yourself as an athlete. I guarantee you it will change the way you stand, the way you walk, and the decisions you make about your body.

MARIAH BURTON NELSON

Do what you can, with what you have, where you are.

THEODORE ROOSEVELT

You were born an original. Don't die a copy.

JOHN MASON

LEARN TO FORGIVE
LET 'ER RIP
LIFE'S JOURNEY

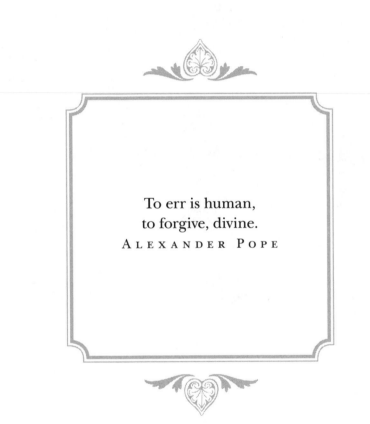

To err is human,
to forgive, divine.

ALEXANDER POPE

Without forgiveness life is governed by...
an endless cycle of resentment and retaliation.
ROBERTO ASSAGIOLI

Resentment is one burden that is incompatible with your
success. Always be the first to forgive; and forgive yourself
first always.
DAN ZADRA

He that cannot forgive others breaks the bridge
over which he must pass himself;
for every man has need to be forgiven.
THOMAS FULLER

If you haven't forgiven yourself something,
how can you forgive others?
DOLORES HUERTA

Forgive, and ye shall be forgiven.
LUKE 6:37

When a deep injury is done us,
we never recover until we forgive.
ALAN PATON

To carry a grudge is like being stung to death by one bee.
WILLIAM H. WALTON

We...need to be able to forgive, because if we don't,
we put our foot right down on the hose of our life force.
SUE PATTON THOELE

To be wronged is nothing unless you
continue to remember it.
CONFUCIUS

When a man points a finger at someone else,
he should remember that three of his fingers
are pointing at himself.
ANONYMOUS

Keeping score of old scores and scars, getting even
and one-upping, always make you less than you are.
MALCOLM FORBES

Any man can seek revenge;
it takes a king or prince to grant a pardon.
ARTHUR J. REHRAT

Anger makes you smaller, while forgiveness
forces you to grow beyond what you were.
CHÉRIE CARTER-SCOTT

Always forgive your enemies—
nothing annoys them so much.
OSCAR WILDE

Forgiveness is a funny thing.
It warms the heart and cools the sting.
WILLIAM ARTHUR WARD

Forgiveness means letting go of the past.
GERALD JAMPOLSKY

One forgives to the degree that one loves.
LA ROCHEFOUCAULD

Forgiveness is the final form of love.
REINHOLD NIEBUHR

Life is an adventure in forgiveness.
NORMAN COUSINS

I don't want to get to the end of my life
and find that I lived just the length of it.
I want to have lived the width of it as well.
DIANE ACKERMAN

Life is a great big canvas, and you should
throw all the paint on it you can.
DANNY KAYE

Life is a paradise for those who love many
things with a passion.
LEO BUSCAGLIA

Live all you can; it's a mistake not to. It doesn't so much
matter what you do in particular, so long as you have
your life. If you haven't had that, what have you had?
HENRY JAMES

The chief danger in life is that you may
take too many precautions.

ALFRED ADLER

Why not upset the apple cart?
If you don't, the apples will rot anyway.

FRANK A. CLARK

I decided long ago never to look at the right hand
of the menu or the price tag of clothes—
otherwise I would starve, naked.

HELEN HAYES

Everybody knows if you are too careful you
are so occupied in being careful that you are
sure to stumble over something.

GERTRUDE STEIN

If you wait for the perfect moment when all is safe
and assured, it may never arrive. Mountains will not
be climbed, races won, or lasting happiness achieved.

MAURICE CHEVALIER

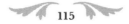

A ship in harbor is safe—
but that is not what ships are for.
JOHN A. SHEDD

Living at risk is jumping off the cliff
and building your wings on the way down.
RAY BRADBURY

Seize the day, put no trust in tomorrow.
HORACE

Live as you will have wished to have
lived when you are dying.
CHRISTIAN F. GELLERT

At the end, you're posing for eternity.
It's your last picture.
Don't be carried into death. Leap into it.
ANATOLE BROYARD

May you live all the days of your life.
JONATHAN SWIFT

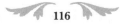

Life is ours to be spent, not to be saved.
D. H. LAWRENCE

Oh, the wild joys of living!
ROBERT BROWNING

If you ask me what I came into this world
to do, I will tell you: I came to live out loud.
EMILE ZOLA

Behold the tortoise. He makes progress only
when he sticks his neck out.
JAMES B. CONANT

Shoot for the moon. Even if you miss it
you will land among the stars.
LES BROWN

Mama exhorted her children at every opportunity
to "jump at the sun." We might not land on
the sun, but at least we would get off the ground.
ZORA NEALE HURSTON

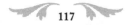

Work like you don't need money,
Love like you've never been hurt,
Sing as if no one can hear you,
And dance like no one's watching.

ANONYMOUS

Nobody cares if you
can't dance well.
Just get up and dance.
DAVE BARRY

Have a blast while you last.
HOLLIS STACY

When you're skating on thin ice,
you may as well tap-dance.
BRYCE COURTENAY

Don't be afraid your life will end;
be afraid that it will never begin.
GRACE HANSEN

The tragedy of man is what dies inside
himself while he still lives.
ALBERT SCHWEITZER

First I was dying to finish high school and start college.
And then I was dying to finish college and start working.
And then I was dying to marry and have children. And
then I was dying for my children to grow old enough so I
could return to work. And then I was dying to retire. And
now, I am dying...and suddenly realize I forgot to live.
ANONYMOUS

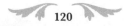

One of the most tragic things I know about human
nature is that all of us tend to put off living. We are
all dreaming of some magical rose garden over the
horizon—instead of enjoying the roses blooming outside
our windows today.

DALE CARNEGIE

Don't hurry, don't worry. You're only here for a
short visit. So be sure to stop and smell the flowers.

WALTER HAGEN

It's only when we truly know and understand
that we have a limited time on earth—and that we have
no way of knowing when our time is up—
that we will begin to live each day to the fullest, as if it
was the only one we had.

ELISABETH KÜBLER-ROSS

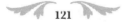

Live each day as you would climb a mountain....
Climb slowly, steadily, enjoying each passing moment;
and the view from the summit will serve as a
fitting climax for the journey.
HAROLD V. MELCHERT

When a child is born, all rejoice; when someone dies,
all weep. But it makes just as much sense, if not more, to
rejoice at the end of a life as at the beginning. For no one
can tell what events await a newborn child, but when a
mortal dies he has successfully completed a journey.
TALMUD

We don't receive wisdom; we must discover it for ourselves
after a journey that no one can take for us or spare us.
MARCEL PROUST

Either control your own destiny, or someone else will!
JOHN F. WELCH, JR.

Destiny is not a matter of chance, it is a matter of choice;
it is not a thing to be waited for, it a thing to be achieved.
WILLIAM JENNINGS BRYAN

We must be willing to get rid of the life we've
planned, so as to have the life that is waiting for us.
JOSEPH CAMPBELL

If we trust our intuition and respond, it's always right,
because we're open enough to see what to do.
PAUL HORN

Every person, all the events of your life are there because
you have drawn them there. What you choose to do with
them is up to you.
RICHARD BACH

The greatest use of life is to spend it
for something that will outlast it.
WILLIAM JAMES

Here is a test to find whether your mission
on earth is finished: if you're alive, it isn't.
RICHARD BACH

The game of life is not so much in holding a
good hand as playing a poor hand well.
H. T. LESLIE

All the art of living lies in a fine mingling
of letting go and holding on.
HAVELOCK ELLIS

Life is a movie you see through your own, unique eyes.
It makes little difference what's happening out there. It's
how you take it that counts.
DENIS WAITLEY

Life moves pretty fast; if you don't stop and look
around every once in a while, you could miss it.
JOHN HUGHES

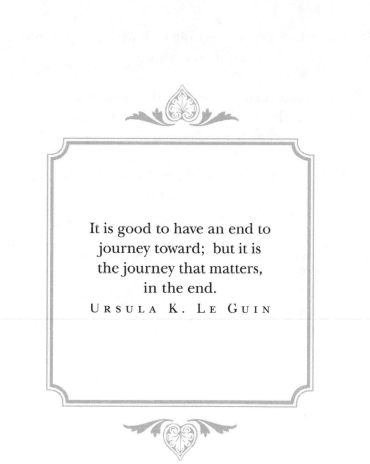

It is good to have an end to
journey toward; but it is
the journey that matters,
in the end.

U R S U L A   K .   L E   G U I N

Life is like a sewer—you get out of it what you put into it.
T O M   L E H R E R

Things turn out best for the people who
make the best of the way things turn out.
J O H N   W O O D E N

Life doesn't require that we do
the best—only that we try our best.
H .   J A C K S O N   B R O W N ,   J R .

Life does not have to be perfect to be wonderful.
A N N E T T E   F U N I C E L L O

NEVER GIVE UP

When things go wrong, as they sometimes will,
when the road you're trudging seems all up hill,
…when care is pressing you down a bit,
rest, if you must—but don't you quit.

ANONYMOUS

Be like a postage stamp—
stick to one thing till you get there.

JOSH BILLINGS

If you really want something, you can
figure out how to make it happen.

CHER

Don't give up when you still have something to give.
Nothing is really over until the moment you stop trying.

BRIAN DYSON

You may be disappointed if you fail,
but you are doomed if you don't try.

BEVERLY SILLS

The important thing is to learn a
lesson every time you lose.
J O H N   M c E N R O E

Problems are messages.
S H A K T I   G A W A I N

A setback is the opportunity to
begin again more intelligently.
H E N R Y   F O R D

Giving up is the ultimate tragedy.
R O B E R T   J .   D O N O V A N

It is common sense to take a method and try it.
If it fails, admit it frankly and try another.
But above all, try something.
F R A N K L I N   D .   R O O S E V E L T

Never let your head hang down. Never give
up and sit down and grieve. Find another way.
S A T C H E L   P A I G E

Fall seven times,
stand up eight.

JAPANESE PROVERB

Our greatest glory is not in never
falling, but in rising every time we fall.
CONFUCIUS

A bend in the road is not the end of the
road…unless you fail to make the turn.
ANONYMOUS

If you have made mistakes there is always another
chance. You may have a fresh start any moment you
choose, for this thing we call "failure" is not the falling
down, but the staying down.
MARY PICKFORD

I think a hero is an ordinary individual who finds the
strength to persevere and endure in spite of
overwhelming obstacles.
CHRISTOPHER REEVE

Keep on keepin' on.
POPULAR SAYING

Little by little does the trick.
AESOP

By perseverance the snail reached the ark.
CHARLES HADDON SPURGEON

In the confrontation between the stream and the rock,
the stream always wins…not through strength, but
through persistence.
ANONYMOUS

The flower that follows the sun does
so even on cloudy days.
ROBERT LEIGHTON

Even the woodpecker owes his success to the fact that
he uses his head and keeps pecking away
until he finishes the job he starts.
COLEMAN COX

Adopt the pace of nature: her secret is patience.
RALPH WALDO EMERSON

The key to everything is patience. You get the
chicken by hatching the egg—not by smashing it.
ARNOLD GLASOW

With time and patience the mulberry
leaf becomes a silk gown.
CHINESE PROVERB

I think and think for months and years.
Ninety-nine times, the conclusion is false.
The hundredth time I am right.
ALBERT EINSTEIN

Champions keep playing until they get it right.
BILLIE JEAN KING

It's easy to have faith in yourself and have discipline
when you're a winner, when you're number one. What
you got to have is faith and discipline
when you're not a winner.
VINCE LOMBARDI

Never confuse a single defeat with a final defeat.
F. SCOTT FITZGERALD

It's never too late, in fiction or in life, to revise.
NANCY THAYER

Overcoming obstacles

Sometimes things which at the moment may be perceived
as obstacles—and actually be obstacles, difficulties,
or drawbacks—can in the long run result in
some good end which would not have occurred
if it had not been for the obstacle.

STEVE ALLEN

The world is round, and the place which may
seem like the end may also be only the beginning.

GEORGE BAKER

What the caterpillar calls the end of the world, the
master calls a butterfly.

RICHARD BACH

Difficulties are meant to rouse, not discourage.
The human spirit is to grow strong by conflict.

WILLIAM ELLERY CHANNING

Adversity causes some men to break;
others to break records.

WILLIAM ARTHUR WARD

I would never have amounted to anything were it not
for adversity. I was forced to come up the hard way.

J. C. PENNEY

I have found that life persists in the midst of
destruction and, therefore, there must be a higher
law than that of destruction.

MAHATMA GANDHI

Life is a series of experiences, each one of which makes
us bigger, even though sometimes it's hard to realize this.

HENRY FORD

The difficulties, hardships and trials of life, the obstacles...are positive blessings. They knit the muscles more
firmly, and teach self-reliance.

WILLIAM MATTHEW

Should you shield the canyons from the windstorms,
you would never see the beauty of their carvings.

ELISABETH KÜBLER-ROSS

The more the marble wastes, the more the statue grows.

MICHELANGELO

If all our misfortunes were laid in one common heap
whence everyone must take an equal portion, most
people would be contented to take their own and depart.

SOCRATES

The more you try to avoid suffering, the more you
suffer because smaller things begin to torture you
in proportion to your fear of suffering.

THOMAS MERTON

To live is to suffer,
to survive is to find meaning in suffering.

VIKTOR FRANKL

Even in the deepest sinking there is the
hidden purpose of an ultimate rising. Thus it is
for all men; from none is the source of light withheld
unless he himself withdraws from it. Therefore
the most important thing is not to despair.

HASIDIC SAYING

Don't get hung up on a snag in the stream, my dear.
Snags alone are not so dangerous—it's the debris that
clings to them that makes the trouble.
Pull yourself loose and go on.

ANNE SHANNON MONROE

Anyone can carry his burden, however heavy, until night-
fall. Anyone can do his work, however hard, for one day.
Anyone can live sweetly, patiently, lovingly, purely, till the
sun goes down and that is all that life really means.

ROBERT LOUIS STEVENSON

Nothing happens to anybody which he is
not fitted by nature to bear.

MARCUS AURELIUS

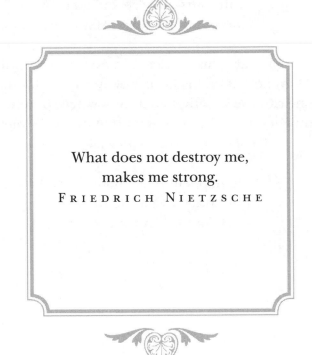

What does not destroy me,
makes me strong.

FRIEDRICH NIETZSCHE

No tree becomes rooted and study unless
many a wind assails it. For by its very tossing
it tightens its grip and plants its roots more securely;
the fragile trees are those that have grown
in a sunny valley.

SENECA

Nothing splendid has ever been achieved except
by those who dared believe that something inside
them was superior to circumstance.

BRUCE BARTON

I seldom think about my limitations, and they never
make me sad. Perhaps there is just a touch of yearning
at times; but it is vague, like a breeze among flowers.

HELEN KELLER

They never told me I couldn't.

TOM DEMPSEY

Some misfortunes we bring upon ourselves;
others are completely beyond our control.
But no matter what happens to us, we always have
some control over what we do about it.

Suzy Szasz

The longer we dwell on our misfortunes,
the greater is their power to harm us.

Voltaire

Trouble is a part of life, and if you don't share it,
you don't give the person who loves you enough
chance to love you enough.

Dinah Shore

It's easy enough to be pleasant when everything goes
like a song, but the man who is worthwhile is the
man who can smile when everything goes dead wrong.

Anonymous

Weeping may endure for a night,
but joy cometh in the morning.

Psalms 30:5

The only way to get through whatever
olympics we're engaged in is by firing up a
sense of humor and pressing on.

JAMES KIRKWOOD

We become so overwhelmed by illness, death,
and grief that we forget that humor, like the moon,
can bring light to our darkest times.

ALLEN KLEIN

By their merry talk they cause sufferers to forget grief.

TALMUD

Turn your stumbling blocks into stepping stones.

ANONYMOUS

Knock the "t" off the can't.

GEORGE REEVES

We are continually faced by great opportunities
brilliantly disguised as insoluble problems.

LEE IACOCCA

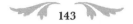

There are no great people in this world, only great
challenges which ordinary people rise to meet.
WILLIAM FREDERICK HALSEY, JR.

Trouble is only opportunity in work clothes.
HENRY J. KAISER

I will love the light for it shows me the way. Yet I
will endure the darkness for it shows me the stars.
OG MANDINO

Do not think of today's failures, but of the
success that may come tomorrow. You have set
yourselves a difficult task, but you will succeed
if you persevere; and you will find a joy in
overcoming obstacles.
HELEN KELLER

Achieving goals by themselves will never make
us happy in the long term: it's who you become, as you
overcome the obstacles necessary to achieve your
goals, that can give you the deepest and most
long-lasting sense of fulfillment.
TONY ROBBINS

Difficult times have helped me to understand
better than before how infinitely rich and
beautiful life is in every way and that so many
things that one goes worrying about are of
no importance whatsoever.

ISAK DINESEN

If you break your neck, if you have nothing to eat,
if your house is on fire—then you've got a problem.
Everything else is inconvenience.

ROBERT FULGHUM

RIGHT LIVELIHOOD

Your work is to discover your work and
then with all your heart to give yourself to it.

THE BUDDHA

The first step is to find out what you love—and don't be
practical about it. The second step is to start doing
what you love immediately, in any small way possible.

BARBARA SHER

All work is empty save when there is love.

KAHLIL GIBRAN

To love what you do and feel that it matters—
how could anything else be more fun?

KATHARINE GRAHAM

Where our work is, there let our joy be.

TERTULLIAN

A musician must make music, an artist must paint,
a poet must write, if he is to be ultimately at peace
with himself. What a man can be, he must be.

ABRAHAM MASLOW

Blessed is he who has found his work.
THOMAS CARLYLE

Every individual has a place to fill in the world
and is important in some respect whether he
chooses to be so or not.
NATHANIEL HAWTHORNE

Work is love made visible. And if you cannot
work with love but only with distaste, it is better
that you should leave your work and sit at the gate
of the temple and take alms of those
who work with joy.
KAHLIL GIBRAN

God gave man work, not to burden him,
but to bless him, and useful work, willingly,
cheerfully, effectively done,
has always been the finest expression
of the human spirit.
WALTER R. COURTENAY

None of us will ever accomplish anything excellent or commanding except when he listens to this whisper which is heard by him alone.

RALPH WALDO EMERSON

The greatness of work is inside man.

POPE JOHN PAUL II

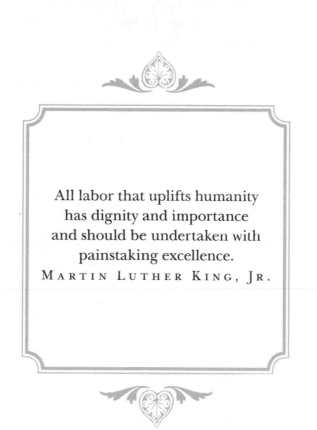

All labor that uplifts humanity
has dignity and importance
and should be undertaken with
painstaking excellence.

MARTIN LUTHER KING, JR.

There is as much dignity in tilling a field
as in writing a poem
BOOKER T. WASHINGTON

There are no menial jobs, only menial attitudes.
WILLIAM J. BENNETT

Honest labor bears a lovely face.
THOMAS DEKKER

I do not like work—no man does—
but I like what is in work—
the chance to find yourself. Your own reality—
for yourself, not for others—
what no other man can ever know.
JOSEPH CONRAD

Life means to have something definite to do—
a mission to fulfill—and in the measure in
which we avoid setting our life to something,
we make it empty. Human life, by its very nature,
has to be dedicated to something.
JOSÉ ORTEGA Y GASSET

Far and away the best prize that life offers is
the chance to work hard at work worth doing.
THEODORE ROOSEVELT

If a man hasn't discovered something
that he would die for, he isn't fit to live.
MARTIN LUTHER KING, JR.

Sometimes it is more important to discover
what one cannot do, than what one can do.
LIN YUTANG

Work is effort applied toward some end. The most
satisfying work involves directing our efforts toward
achieving ends that we ourselves endorse as worthy
expressions of our talent and character.
WILLIAM J. BENNETT

Let us not be content to wait and see what
will happen, but give us the determination to
make the right things happen.
PETER MARSHALL

The return from your work must be the satisfaction
which that work brings you and the world's need of that
work. With that, life is heaven, or as near heaven as you
can get. Without this—with work which you despise,
which bores you, and which the world does not need—
this life is hell.

W. E. B. Du Bois

We become what we do.

Chiang Kai-Shek

It's no good running a pig farm badly for
thirty years while saying, "Really I was meant
to be a ballet dancer." By that time,
pigs will be your style.

Quentin Crisp

Let each man pass his days in that
wherein his skill is greatest.

Sextus Propertius

Destiny is what you are supposed to do in life.
Fate is what kicks you in the ass to make you do it.

Henry Miller

Work has to include our deepest values
and passions and feelings and commitments,
or it's not work, it's just a job.
MATTHEW FOX

Anybody can do just about anything with himself that
he really wants to and makes up his mind to do. We are
capable of greater things than we realize.
NORMAN VINCENT PEALE

Do what you love, the money will follow
MARSHA SINETAR

SWEET SMELL OF SUCCESS

Don't aim for success if you want it; just do what
you love and believe in, and it will come naturally.
DAVID FROST

Success follows doing what you want to do.
There is no other way to be successful.
MALCOLM FORBES

Know what you want to do, hold the thought firmly,
and do every day what should be done, and
every sunset will see you that much nearer the goal.
ELBERT HUBBARD

Every successful person I have heard of has done the best
he could with the conditions as he found them, and not
waited until next year for better.
E. W. HOWE

It takes twenty years to make an overnight success.
EDDIE CANTOR

Perseverance is a great element of success.
If you only knock long enough and loud enough at the
gate, you are sure to wake up somebody.
HENRY WADSWORTH LONGFELLOW

The elevator to success is out of order. You'll
have to use the stairs…one step at a time.
JOE GIRARD

Success seems to be largely a matter of
hanging on after others have let go.
WILLIAM FEATHER

Most people who succeed in the face of
seemingly impossible conditions are people
who simply don't know how to quit.
ROBERT SCHULLER

Character cannot be developed in ease and quiet.
Only through experience of trial and
suffering can the soul be strengthened,
ambition inspired, and success achieved.
HELEN KELLER

I cannot give you the formula for success,
but I can give you the formula for failure, which is:
try to please everybody.
HERBERT B. SWOPE

You always pass failure on the way to success.
MICKEY ROONEY

If you're not failing now and again,
it's a sign you're playing it safe.
WOODY ALLEN

The difference between good and great
is just a little extra effort.
DUFFY DAUGHERTY

If you aren't going all the way, why go at all?
JOE NAMATH

Success is not the result of spontaneous combustion.
You must first set yourself on fire.
FRED SHERO

People become really quite remarkable when they start
thinking that they can do things. When they believe
in themselves they have the first secret of success.
NORMAN VINCENT PEALE

While one person hesitates because he feels inferior, the
other is busy making mistakes and becoming superior.
HENRY C. LINK

I studied the lives of great men and famous women, and
I found that the men and women who get to the top were
those who did the jobs they had in hand, with everything
they had of energy and enthusiasm and hard work.
HARRY S. TRUMAN

Keep away from people who try to belittle your
ambitions. Small people always do that, but the really
great make you feel that you, too, can become great.
MARK TWAIN

Whenever you're sitting across from some important
person, always picture him sitting there in a suit of long
underwear. That's the way I always operated in business.
JOSEPH P. KENNEDY

Everything depends upon circumstances:
you must sail according to the wind.
PICONNERIE DE LA BUGEAUD

Don't wait for your ship to come; swim out to it.
ANONYMOUS

Find a need and fill it.
HENRY J. KAISER

The secret to success in life is for a man to be
ready for his opportunity when it comes.
BENJAMIN DISRAELI

If a window of opportunity appears
don't pull down the shade.
TOM PETERS

If opportunity doesn't knock, build a door.
MILTON BERLE

Don't be afraid to take a big step if one is indicated.
You can't cross a chasm in two small jumps.
DAVID LLOYD GEORGE

There are some things one can only achieve
by a deliberate leap in the opposite direction.

FRANZ KAFKA

Why should we be in such desperate haste to succeed,
and in such desperate enterprises? If a man does not
keep pace with his companions, perhaps it is because he
hears a different drummer.

HENRY DAVID THOREAU

Success consists of getting up just
one more time than you fall.

OLIVER GOLDSMITH

Genius is one percent inspiration and ninety-nine
percent perspiration.

THOMAS A. EDISON

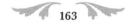

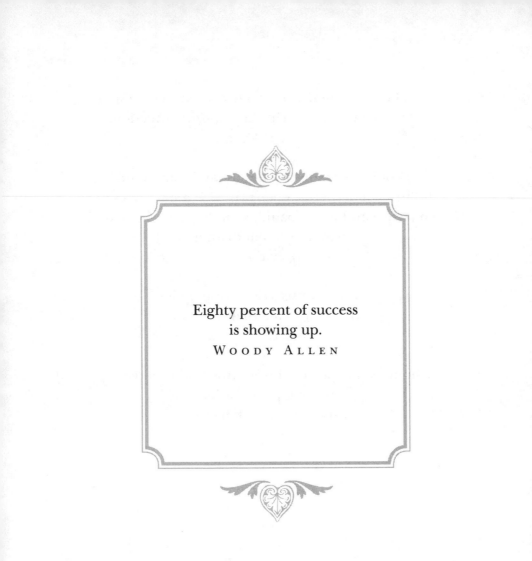

Eighty percent of success
is showing up.

WOODY ALLEN

The secret of success is constancy to purpose.
BENJAMIN DISRAELI

The world stands aside to let anyone
pass who knows where he is going.
DAVID STARR JORDAN

Winners can tell you where they are going,
what they plan to do along the way,
and who will be sharing the adventure with them.
DENIS WAITLEY

Success means we go to sleep at night knowing that our
talents and abilities were used in a way that served others.
MARIANNE WILLIAMSON

If a man has a talent and cannot use it,
he has failed. If he has a talent and uses only
half of it, he has partially failed. If he has a talent
and learns somehow to use the whole of it,
he has gloriously succeeded, and won a satisfaction
and a triumph few men ever know.
THOMAS WOLFE

The richest person is the one
who is contented with what he has.
ROBERT C. SAVAGE

Abundance is about being rich,
with or without money.
SUZE ORMAN

Money may be the husk of many things,
but not the kernel. It brings you food,
but not appetite; medicine, but not health;
acquaintances, but not friends; servants, but not loyalty;
days of joy, but not peace or happiness.
HENRIK IBSEN

He has achieved success who has lived well,
laughed often, and loved much.
ELBERT HUBBARD

No man is a failure who is enjoying life.
WILLIAM FEATHER

I'd rather be a failure at something I enjoy
than be a success at something I hate.

GEORGE BURNS

Most people can do extraordinary things if
they have the confidence or take the risks.
Yet most people don't. They sit in front of the
telly and treat life as if it goes on forever.

PHILLIP ADAMS

God gave us two ends. One to sit on and one to think
with. Success depends on which one you use;
heads, you win—tails, you lose.

ANONYMOUS

TAKE THE FIRST STEP

A journey of a thousand miles must
begin with a single step.
CHINESE PROVERB

What saves a man is to take a step.
Then another step.
ANTOINE DE SAINT-EXUPÉRY

The distance is nothing.
It's only the first step that's important.
MARQUISE DU DEFFAND

He who has begun has half done.
Dare to be wise; begin!
HORACE

Begin somewhere; you cannot build a
reputation on what you intend to do.
LIZ SMITH

No matter how big or soft or warm
your bed is, you still have to get out of it.
GRACE SLICK

The beginning is the most important part of the work.

P L A T O

Don't wait for something big to occur. Start where you are, with what you have, and that will always lead you into something greater.

M A R Y   M A N I N   M O R R I S S E Y

The person who moves a mountain begins by carrying away small stones.

CHINESE PROVERB

The older I get, the more wisdom I find in the
ancient rule of taking first things first—a process
which often reduces the most complex human problems
to manageable proportions.
DWIGHT D. EISENHOWER

The secret of getting ahead is getting started. The
secret of getting started is breaking your complex overwhelming tasks into small manageable tasks, and then
starting on the first one.
MARK TWAIN

You can't try to do things; you simply must do them.
RAY BRADBURY

The tragedy of life is not that it ends so
soon, but that we wait so long to begin it.
ANONYMOUS

Inaction may be the biggest form of action.
JERRY BROWN

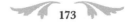

If you don't know where you are going,
you will probably end up somewhere else.

LAURENCE J. PETER

The important thing is somehow to begin.

HENRY MOORE

As long as you can start, you are all right.
The juice will come.

ERNEST HEMINGWAY

Often people attempt to live their lives backwards;
they try to have more things, or more money,
in order to do more of what they want,
so they will be happier. The way it actually
works is the reverse. You must first be who you
really are, then do what you need to do,
in order to have what you want.

MARGARET YOUNG

Knowing what you want is the first step to getting it.

LOUISE HART

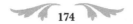

Where we stand is not as important as the
direction in which we are going.

OLIVER WENDELL HOLMES, JR.

If you're climbing the ladder of life,
you go rung by rung, one step at a time....
Sometimes you don't think you're progressing
until you step back and see
how high you've really gone.

DONNY OSMOND

Never look down to test the ground before
taking your next step; only he who keeps his
eye fixed on the far horizon will find his right road.

DAG HAMMARSKJÖLD

"Begin at the beginning," the king said, gravely,
"and go till you come to the end; then stop."

LEWIS CARROLL

WIN SOME, LOSE SOME

You're gonna lose some
ballgames and you're gonna
win some ballgames
and that's about it.

SPARKY ANDERSON

For everything you have missed,
you have gained something else;
and for everything you gain, you lose something.
RALPH WALDO EMERSON

Sometimes things can go right
only by first going very wrong.
EDWARD TENNER

There are many in this old world of ours
who hold that things break about even for all of us.
I have observed for example that we all get the same
amount of ice. The rich get it in the summertime
and the poor get it in the winter.
BAT MASTERSON

Life is pretty simple: you do some stuff. Most fails.
Some works. You do more of what works. If it works big,
others quickly copy it. Then you do something else.
The trick is the doing something else.
TOM PETERS

Victory is not won in miles but in inches. Win a little
now, hold your ground, and later win a little more.
LOUIS L'AMOUR

If you think you can win, you can win.
Faith is necessary to victory
WILLIAM HAZLITT

Pick battles big enough to matter,
small enough to win.
JONATHAN KOZOL

If it was a worthwhile fight, it didn't matter
who won; some good was sure to come of it.
RICHARD BROOKS

When you let someone else win an
argument, often you both end up winners.
RICHARD CARLSON

The person who upsets you the most is your best teacher,
because they bring you face to face with who you are.
LYNN ANDREWS

Some people like me. Some people don't.
You can never get everyone to like you,
so why knock yourself out trying?
CLAUDETTE COLBERT

Winners never quit and quitters never win.
VINCE LOMBARDI

You really never lose until you stop trying.
MIKE DITKA

Everything that has a beginning has an ending.
Make your peace with that and all will be well.
THE BUDDHA

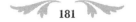

INDEX

ABOUT THE AUTHOR

ALLEN KLEIN is an award-winning professional speaker and best-selling author. He is a recipient of a Lifetime Achievement Award from the Association for Applied and Therapeutic Humor, a Certified Speaking Professional designation from the National Speakers Association, and a Communication and Leadership Award from Toastmasters International. He is also an inductee in the Hunter College, New York City, Hall of Fame and the author of fifteen books.

For more information about Klein's books or presentations, visit www.allenklein.com or contact him at allen@allenklein.com

To Our Readers

Viva Editions publishes books that inform, enlighten, and entertain. We do our best to bring you, the reader, quality books that celebrate life, inspire the mind, revive the spirit, and enhance lives all around. Our authors are practical visionaries: people who offer deep wisdom in a hopeful and helpful manner. Viva was launched with an attitude of growth and we want to spread our joy and offer our support and advice where we can to help you live the Viva way: vivaciously!

We're grateful for all our readers and want to keep bringing you books for inspired living. We invite you to write to us with your comments and suggestions, and what you'd like to see more of. You can also sign up for our online newsletter to learn about new titles, author events, and special offers.

Viva Editions
2246 Sixth St.
Berkeley, CA 94710
www.vivaeditions.com
(800) 780-2279
Follow us on Twitter @vivaeditions
Friend/fan us on Facebook